If there is one word that is the byword of all magicians that word would have to be SECRECY. In the foreword of every book ever written by a magician, the reader is always constrained never ever to reveal a trick's secrets. The reader is told that this is some sort of unwritten but nevertheless inviolate magician's code. And somehow, this code is honored by millions of readers of millions of books that show how millions of tricks are done.

But, as far as we are concerned, this is all nonsense. Our tricks do not need to be kept secret. Our tricks do not have to be hidden. Our tricks do not have to be reserved for a chosen few. Why . . . ? Why do we fly in the face of tradition? Because our tricks do not work, that is why.

Anyway, we just don't go in for silly codes and restrictions. Go ahead and tell anyone whatever you want from this book. Tell them all you like to your heart's content. Just one little thing we ask you not to do with this book. Don't lend it! Lending means not buying. Not buying means that not only won't the tricks in this book work, but the author of the book won't work either.

And now on to this entertaining, engrossing, fascinating, and often diverting volume about which one reviewer said, "Once you've started reading, you'll certainly want to put it down."

THE MAD BOOK OF MAGIC AND OTHER DIRTY TRICKS

Written and Illustrated by

AL JAFFEE

Edited by

Jerry De Fuccio

Ⓢ

A SIGNET BOOK

NEW AMERICAN LIBRARY

TIMES MIRROR

New York and Scarborough, Ontario

The New English Library Limited, London

Dedication

To the author of "MAD'S AL JAFFEE SPEWS OUT SNAPPY ANSWERS TO STUPID QUESTIONS", without whose inspired and tireless efforts this book would not have been possible.

SIGNET, SIGNET CLASSICS, MENTOR, PLUME AND MERIDIAN BOOKS
are published *in the United States* by
The New American Library, Inc.,
1301 Avenue of the Americas, New York, New York 10019,
in Canada by The New American Library of Canada Limited,
81 Mack Avenue, Scarborough 704, Ontario,
in the United Kingdom by The New English Library Limited,
Barnard's Inn, Holborn, London, E.C. 1, England

FIRST PRINTING, FEBRUARY, 1970

6 7 8 9 10 11 12 13 14

PRINTED IN THE UNITED STATES OF AMERICA

FOREWORD

is no surprise that when the definitive book on magic was be written, it would be Al Jaffee who would write it. Having raduated Harvard (B.M., M.M.), Jaffee continued to exhaust e Departments of Magic at Yale, Princeton and Hofstra with ost-graduate courses, absorbing all the information available on this critically important subject, and achieving, for the irst time anywhere, the degree of Doctor of Magic!

was Jaffee who was called in to settle the arguments between the irreconcilably split factions of the Zurich Academy f Magical Arts, just as he had done at the Leipzig Conservaory of Magic 200 years earlier (one of his typical magical eats).

was Jaffee, too, who proved to the world that the eye can e quicker than the hand.

nd, of course, it was Jaffee who coined the phrase "You can ead a horse to water, but you can't make him do tricks, exept sometimes," which has become the credo of every important magician today.

nd now this book, the "punctuation ending the sentence of agic that is his life," as Winston Churchill was rumored to ave said, and though others may have said it better, it really oesn't matter. What does matter is that Jaffee *is*, and, when ou stop to think about it, it seems incongruent, but isn't inongruency nine-tenths of the law?

nick meglin

Nick Meglin
Magic Editor
Mad Magazine

CHAPTER ONE

**SIMPLE TRICKS
FOR SIMPLE CLODS
OR...
YOU CAN'T CHEAT
AN HONEST MAN
AND YET WE GOT 60¢
OUT OF YOU
FOR THIS BOOK.
THINK ABOUT THAT,
DUM DUM!**

THE CLASSIC GOOSE LAYING
THE GOLDEN EGG TRICK

MORAL: Don't expect too much from a goose.

Another eggciting chapter to (yecch!) follow.

THE STARTLING
"BUFFALO OUT OF A HAT" TRICK

Tell the audience that you intend to pull a buffalo out of your hat. They will chuckle derisively. But this will soon turn to repentance and astonishment as you proceed to pull a real live prairie buffalo out of your hat as promised.

HOW THE TRICK IS DONE

The hat has a removable top. As you place it on the table, you palm the top and slip it up your sleeve. The hat then goes over a slit in the tablecloth which is over a hole in the table. It is thus a simple matter to reach down and pull out the buffalo concealed inside.

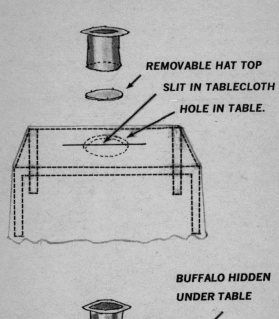

REMOVABLE HAT TOP

SLIT IN TABLECLOTH

HOLE IN TABLE.

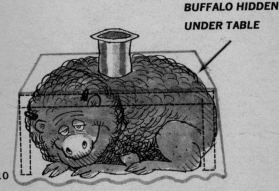

BUFFALO HIDDEN
UNDER TABLE

THE DAMP
"WATER RUNNING UPHILL"
TRICK

Place an ordinary pitcher of water on one side of a table and a shallow receptacle on the other. Tell your audience that you intend to make the water flow up and out of the pitcher and into the shallow receptacle. As you wave your magic wand you offer magic incantations that become louder and louder. Suddenly, as the audience's excitement reaches a polite frenzy, the water miraculously flows **uphill** and into the nearby receptacle.

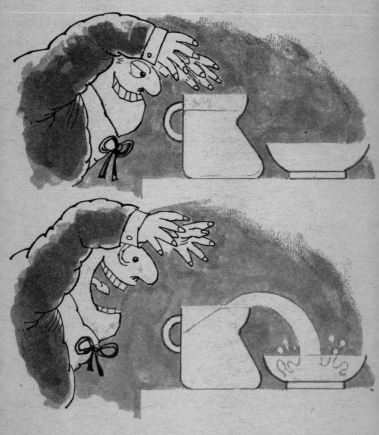

HOW THE TRICK IS DONE

This trick requires extensive preparation beforehand but the results are well worth the time and effort. You will need the services of any local house-moving organization. Have them place electrically operated hydraulic jacks under one side of the house, church, or auditorium in which you are scheduled to perform. Thus, as you begin to build toward the climax of your act, the entire room is slowly tilting. Naturally, to those inside, the table and pitcher seem level. But, they are tilted enough for the water to start flowing and creating the "uphill" illusion. This trick wowed them at the 1969 Cherokee Conjurers Convention in Yankee Stadium.

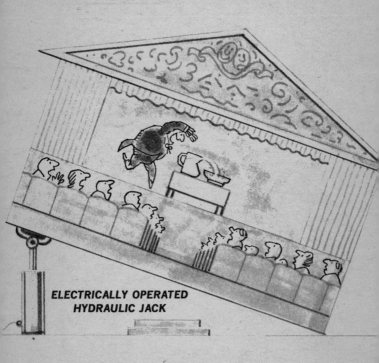

ELECTRICALLY OPERATED HYDRAULIC JACK

THE INCOMPARABLE "TRAVELING WATCH" TRICK

Ask the audience for a watch and hold it in one hand with both hands outstretched. Close your hand on the watch, utter some magic words, and, thirty minutes later, to the audience's complete astonishment, the watch appears in your **other** hand.

THE WATCH

THE WATCH

HOW THE TRICK IS DONE

For this trick, you will require almost two thousand fleas. They are strong and easy to train. In this instance, you must train them to drag the watch into your right sleeve, across your chest, and out your left sleeve. After some practice you will get used to housing two thousand fleas on your person, without feeling you're going to itch yourself to death.

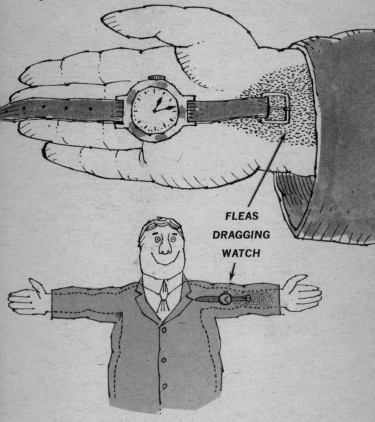

FLEAS
DRAGGING
WATCH

CHAPTER TWO

INTRODUCING

"THE GREAT BUMBLEONI"

OR
IF YOU'RE GOING TO
DO SOMETHING WRONG,
DO IT RIGHT!

CHAPTER THREE

MORE SIMPLE TRICKS
FOR LESS SIMPLE CLODS
OR
WHAT TO DO
UNTIL THE
LOCKSMITH COMES

THE CLASSIC GOOSE LAYING
THE GOLDEN EGG TRICK

MORAL: You can't expect a laugh every time you crack a yolk.

Another eggcellent installment (yucch!) soon.

THE PROLONGED
"WATER EVAPORATION" TRICK

Tell the audience that you can make five gallons of water evaporate into thin air. Then take an ordinary newspaper, shape it into a cone, and hold it aloft so that an assistant can pour five gallons of water into it. To enhance the lightness and gaiety of this particular feat, you might refer to your unsmiling helper as "Gunga Din" or "Water Lou". When the pouring has ceased, intone the magic word "Mo-non-ga-he-la", open the paper cone, and show your transfixed viewers that the water has disappeared. To top that off, the newspaper isn't even wet!

HOW THE TRICK IS DONE

The newspaper must be prepared ahead of time, which is done by simply giving it a good coat of plastic spray. Now, concealed in your sleeve is a funnel attached to a hose which runs to a balloon fitted around your waist. **CAUTION:** Always save this trick for the very last as the sloshing noises you make when you walk may give the trick away. Also, be extremely careful when taking bows as a ruptured balloon can lead the audience to jump to embarrassing conclusions.

THE PRINCELY
"SWALLOWING A LIVE EEL"
TRICK

This is not so much a trick as a bit of divertimento to help warm up the audience. On a table next to you is a fish tank. Tell the audience you forgot to have dinner, heightening their glee by tucking your handkerchief under your chin like a bib, and then reach into the tank and pull out a wildly wriggling eel. You pop the eel into your mouth, and while the audience is still sputtering and choking, tell them how you fooled them with a **rubber eel** which you made **life-like** by wiggling with your fingers. To prove it, you reach into your mouth and extract a limp eel and say, "See, what did I tell you? It's a phony eel". As you are saying this, drop the limp eel into the tank and suddenly it comes to life and swims away, to everyone's bemusement.

HOW THE TRICK IS DONE

The trick is that you do indeed swallow a rubber eel. But, tucked carefully inside your mouth is a **real** ANESTHETIZED eel. When you remove it, it hangs limp and unconscious and you tell everyone it is rubber. However, when dropped into cold water it instantly revives and gives the impression of a rubber eel coming to life. A totally fulfilling and delightfully disarming trick.

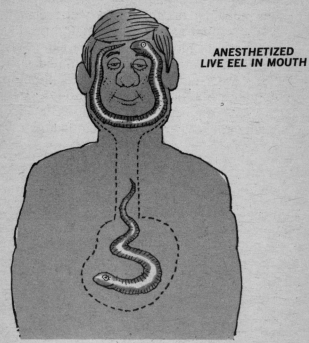

ANESTHETIZED LIVE EEL IN MOUTH

SWALLOWED RUBBER EEL

THE EVER-BAFFLING "ANIMATED OBJECTS" TRICK

Place an ordinary pencil, pliers and nutcracker on a table. Tell your audience that you intend to mass-hypnotize them into believing they are seeing these objects come to life. Their unruly cries of "fat chance!" will soon turn to wonder and adulation as you intone the words "COME ALIVE...!" and snap your fingers simultaneously. Right before their eyes, the pencil starts hopping, the pliers starts snapping, and the nut cracker starts spinning.

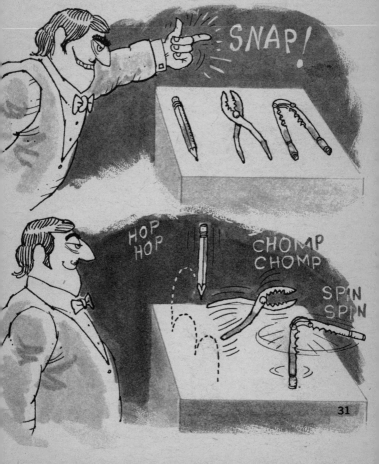

HOW THE TRICK IS DONE

The genius behind this feat is that you do **not** indulge in mass-hypnosis of the audience but you **do** hypnotize each object, about a half hour before going on. You suggest to the pencil that it is actually a kangaroo, that the pliers is an alligator, and that the nutcracker is a ballerina. Then you implant a post-hypnotic suggestion in them before bringing them back to normal, which is whenever they hear the command "COME ALIVE . . .!", and at the snap of your fingers, they will once again act like a kangaroo, an alligator, and a ballerina. A simple but effective trick.

CHAPTER FOUR

THE INCREDIBLE

"IRON STOMACH MAN"

OR

A TOUGH ACT
TO SWALLOW

And now, the CLINCHER . . . the act that took twenty-five years to perfect . . .

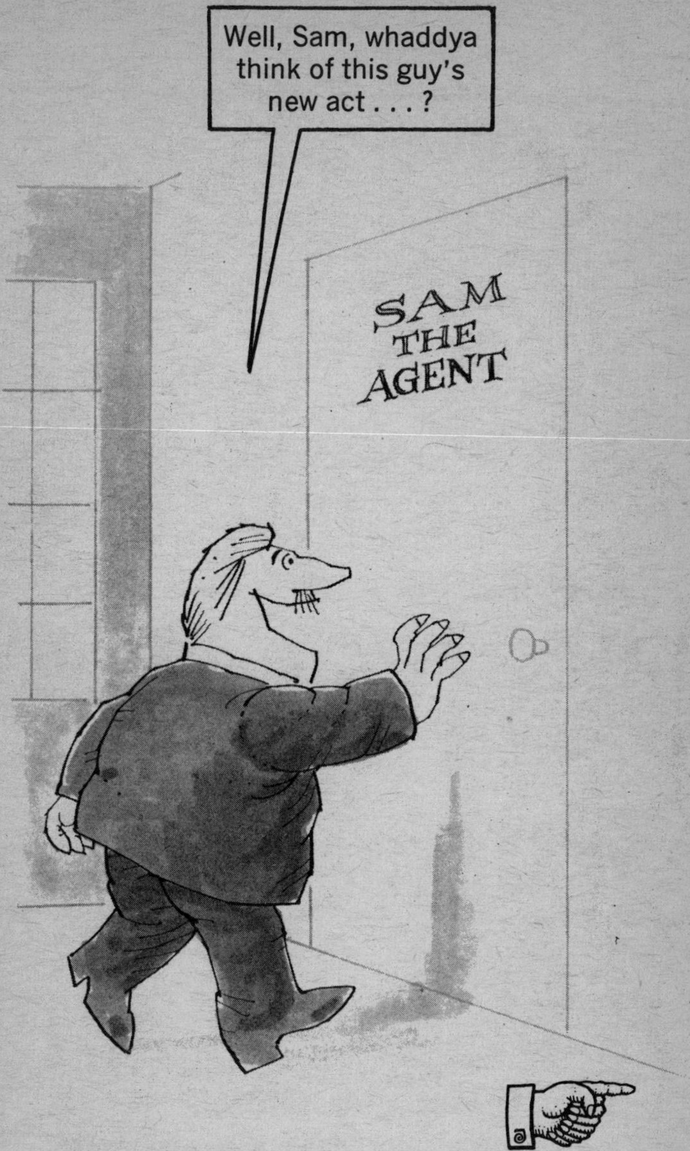
Well, Sam, whaddya think of this guy's new act . . . ?
SAM THE AGENT

THE CORPUSCULAR
"BLOOD FROM A STONE" TRICK

Produce an ordinary stone and let your audience examine it. After they are convinced it is genuine, tell them you intend to squeeze it until blood flows. To their utter astonishment, and disgust, you proceed to cover the stage with blood.

Ordinary stone

HOW THE TRICK IS DONE

Any idiot knows you can't get blood from a stone. If you've heard that once, you've heard it a dozen times. But did you ever hear anyone say, "You can't get blood from a magician...?" That's why they'll never suspect you did it with a quantity of broken glass shards concealed in your hand.

Caution: Remember to inform the Stage Manager of your blood type before each and every performance.

CHAPTER FIVE

"THE GREAT BUMBLEONI"

GESTURES
HYPNOTICALLY
OR
SLAY IT WITH FLOWERS

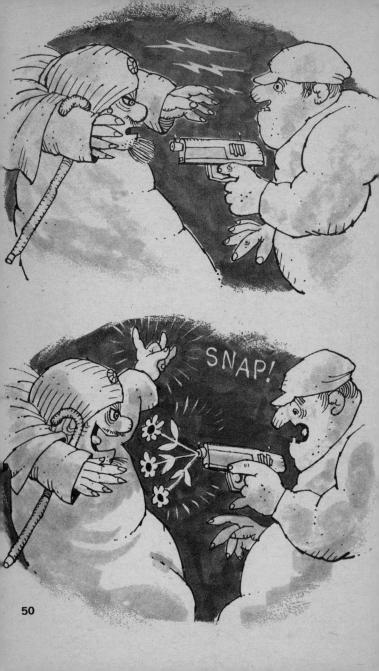

CHAPTER SIX

ADVANCED TRICKS
FOR SIMPLE CLODS
OR
THE HAND IS
QUICKER
THAN THE WRIST

THE CLASSIC GOOSE
LAYING THE GOLDEN EGG TRICK

MORAL: A goose and rooster could produce
a gooster if they didn't chicken out.

More eggshilarating stuff like this (yicch!) to come.

THE FLAGRANT "DISAPPEARING BILL" TRICK

Ask someone in the audience for a ten dollar bill. Hold it up for everyone to see and then with a wave of your magic wand . . . POOF . . . it is gone.

HOW THE TRICK IS DONE

Here is an excellent example of magic wand wielding. The key to this trick is of course **MIS-DIRECTION.** As you hold up the ten dollar bill with one hand, you wave the magic wand with the other, pressing a button that makes sparks fly out of the wand. During the moment that the audience is distracted, you pop the ten dollar bill into your mouth and swallow it. A good follow-up for this trick is the disgusting **"RE-APPEARING TEN DOLLAR BILL" TRICK** but we'd just as soon **(YECCHH!)** skip it, if you don't mind.

THE SWELL
"CHOPPED-OFF FINGER" TRICK

Tell the audience you've never found any use for your pinky finger and you'd like someone to come up and chop it off. From the rush of volunteers, select one and give him a meat cleaver. Place your pinky on the block as shown and let the volunteer chop away.

HOW THE TRICK IS DONE

It is actually true that the pinky finger is expendable and can be removed surgically without impairing manual dexterity. Once this is done, buy a large supply of rubber pinkies which are easily attached to the hand with adhesive. Thus, when you offer your pinky to be chopped off, it is totally painless to you. But remember which hand has the phony otherwise a nasty spectacle will occur onstage.

THE FORCEFUL "BRINGING A ROPE TO LIFE" TRICK

Take a length of rope out of your pocket and place it on the table. Then tell your audience that with two taps of your magic wand you can bring the rope to life, which you proceed to do to the unbridled rapture and acclaim of your viewers.

HOW THE TRICK IS DONE

To begin with, the rope is no ordinary rope. It is a braided piece in which one of the braids has been removed and replaced by a yellow snake of the right length. At each end of the "rope", a tiny thumbtack is concealed. Thus, when you bring the rope out and place it on the table, you are actually pushing down the thumbtacks. Then, when you give the two taps of your magic wand, you are actually knocking each end of the "rope" free from the table, and the snake/rope will slither away.

You might practice first with a string and a worm until you are truly proficient at this convulsing hoax on the people.

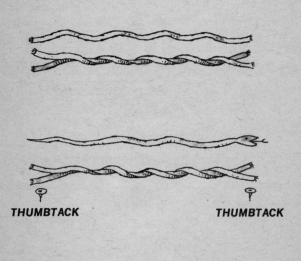

THUMBTACK   **THUMBTACK**

CONCEALED   **CONCEALED**
THUMBTACK   **THUMBTACK**

CHAPTER SEVEN

A MAGICIAN'S GUIDE TO HECKLERS, DOUBTERS AND OTHER VERMIN

Any time a magician starts a trick he can surely count on some idiot to ask a stupid question that ruins his timing, the whole trick, and his return engagement chances. There is only **one way** to deal with this nemesis of legerdemain. To illustrate the way, we will borrow a technique from another informative, educational, and brilliantly conceived book entitled *"**MAD's** Al Jaffee Spews Out Snappy Answers to Stupid Questions". So, here is **SNAPPY ANSWERS TO STUPID MAGIC QUESTIONS.**

*Look for my follow-up book "**MAD's** Al Jaffee Spews Out Snappy Humbleness, Self-Effacement and Acts of Pious Humility"

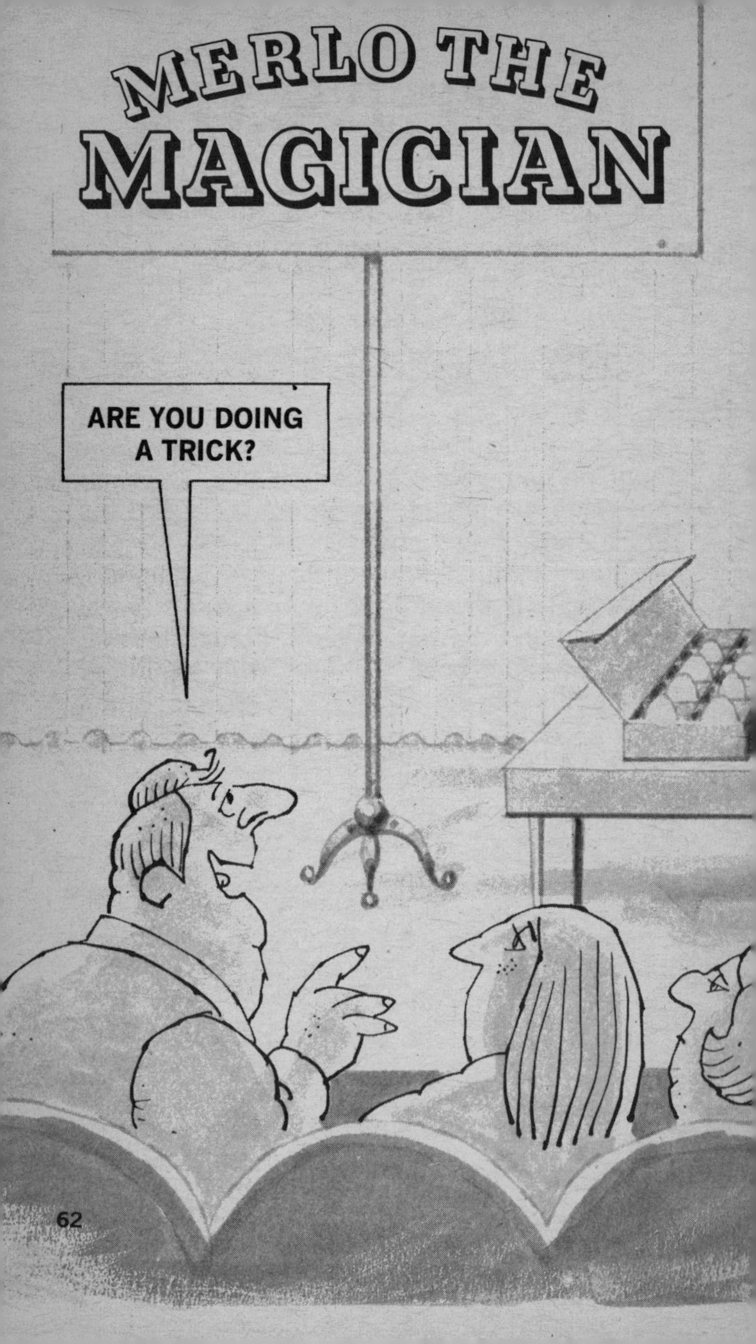
MERLO THE MAGICIAN
ARE YOU DOING A TRICK?

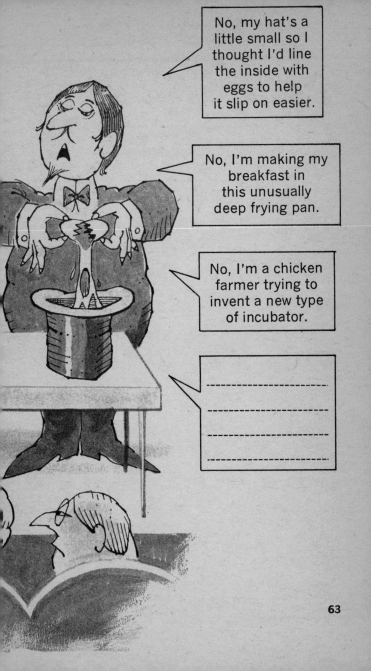

63

No, I'm pulling a lion out of a hat. The rabbit just happens to be caught in his teeth!
No, I'm pulling out the lining which happens to be made of rabbit fur.
No, I'm pulling a hat from around a rabbit.

No,
I'm minding them
for a
friend who **is.**
He asked me not
to lose his place.

No, a bumbler!
I've been trying
to catch
these balls for
fifteen minutes.

No, I'm a
sidewalk
pawnbroker and
this is the only way
I can display
the symbols of
my trade.

THE GREAT

SNAPPY

ANSWERS

TO STUPID

QUESTIONS

PRESTO

CHANGE-O

TRICK

GLITCH!

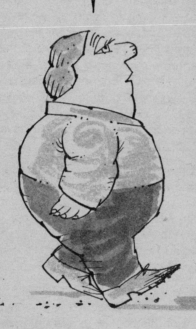

WORLD'S DIRTIEST TRICK

There are some dirty tricks in this book. There are quite a lot of dirty tricks in this book. In fact, this whole book is a dirty trick! But it's too late to do anything about that. You won't get your money back. So, you might as well try and get whatever you can out of the book; a good trick right there!

But, with all the dirty tricks in the book, one stands out above the rest. And you've just had it! Where in the world of publishing have you ever heard of an author who had the unmitigated gall to waste 19 pages of his book to advertise another one of his books . . . ? That's **exactly** what just happened here. The preceding 19 pages were a thinly disguised chapter on magic, a cheap plug for the author's other book, "Snappy Answers to Stupid Questions," available through your bookstore or by mailing 60¢ plus 10¢ (per copy) to cover mailing costs. Check or money order, please. No currency or C.O.D.'s!

New York City residents add 6% sales tax. Other New York State residents add 3% plus any local sales or use taxes. Send to:

> The New American Library, Inc.
> P.O. Box 2310
> Grand Central Station
> New York, New York 10017

Imagine allowing yourself to be tricked like this! Now that you're a well-seasoned dupe, maybe you'll take the rest of this book with a grain of salt.

CHAPTER EIGHT

THE GREAT
BUMBLEONI'S
MAGIC LAMP TRICK
OR
WHAT A WAY TO GLOW

The Great
Magic
Disappearing
Lamp Trick

POOF!

86

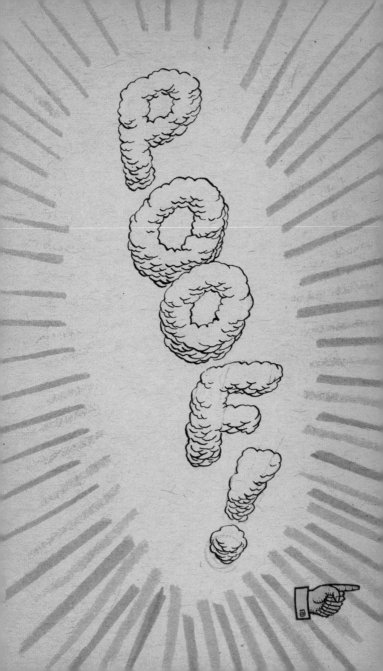

The Great
Magic
Disappearing
Lamp Trick

THE WORLD'S MOST FRUSTRATING TRICK...
REVEALED AT LAST!

This trick has driven millions of people insane through the ages. Its diabolical simplicity utterly defies solution. Well, we have the solution and what's more we are going to share it with you, dear reader. But first, let's reacquaint ourselves with the problem: Arrange nine matchsticks so that they form a perfect square. Remember, no breaking, no overlapping, or any other sneaky tricks.

To end your nightmare of frustration turn to pages 183 and 184 for the relief-giving solution.

CHAPTER NINE

ADVANCED TRICKS
FOR
ADVANCED CLODS

OR

PUT A TIGER
IN YOUR TURBAN

THE CLASSIC GOOSE
LAYING THE GOLDEN EGG TRICK

MORAL: A fool dreams of gold being handed to him on a silver platter.

Still more eggceptional stuff (yocch!) imminent.

You are bound head to toe with chains, ropes, cables, bandages, wire, straps, and Scotch tape. You are then placed in a laundry bag and lowered into a tank of water. As the seconds tick away, the audience becomes more and more anxious and the suspense is strength-sapping. Finally, when the tension is tantamount to teeth-grinding, you emerge . . . **safe** and **sound!** The audience, relieved because that most precious of all things, a human life, did not perish in the tank, will applaud enthusiastically.

HOW THE TRICK IS DONE

Though this is one of the most stupefying tricks of all, it is at the same time the simplest. The key to the whole thing is a midget hidden in the laundry bag. Working swiftly and surely, he unshackles, unwinds and generally releases you just in time for you to avoid drowning. An even better trick would be to figure out how to keep the midget from drowning. Maybe someday someone will! Meanwhile, the supply of midgets is quite plentiful.*

* CONSULT "MIDGET MART" IN YOUR YELLOW PAGES.

THE BREATH-TAKING "HUNG BY THE NECK" TRICK

Tell your audience that you have learned muscle control to such a degree you can survive being hanged for an hour without ill effect. You then mount a scaffold and are hanged in the standard procedure. To heighten the dramatic impact, scream, choke, gurgle, roll your eyes and generally make the hideous and disgusting noises associated with a hanging. After dangling limply for awhile, abruptly flop your head to one side and pop out your tongue as if dead. Then, after the fainters and retchers in your audience have been revived and cleaned up, suddenly spring to life as good as new!

HOW THE TRICK IS DONE

You will need a twelve inch length of steel pipe for this trick. After a little practice, you will learn to swallow it with the ease of a sword-swallower. Thus, when the noose tightens around your neck, your windpipe will not close completely and you can go on breathing. All that choking, gurgling, and disgusting noisemaking is just an act.

Proof once again that the best tricks are the simple tricks!

THE EDIFYING
"EDUCATED ROPE" TRICK

Grasp a two foot length of rope and snap it like a whip. Miraculously, it will knot itself. Another snap and it unknots itself. Your audience will be ecstatic and bright-eyed at this feat.

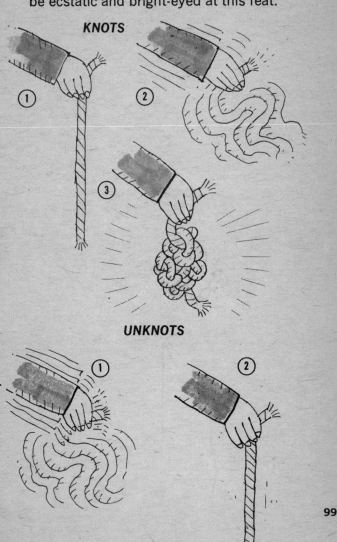

KNOTS

UNKNOTS

HOW THE TRICK IS DONE

Practice is the key to this trick. The following illustrations in slow motion show exactly what you must learn to do.

At start of trick, all fingers of rope hand must touch rope.

During snap, twist rope 3/8 inch to right and hold 2/9 second.

As rope starts upward, bend wrist down 47 degrees for 1/19 second.

As rope makes first knotting approach, tweak it gently with pinky.

As rope goes into second knotting approach, snap index finger.

Finally, spin thumb in a 3/4 inch arc and trick is all finished.

To Unknot: Simply Reverse Above Procedure

CHAPTER TEN

RIDICULOUS RIDDLES, POINTLESS PUZZLES, AND GHASTLY GAMES
OR
FUN FOR THE WHOLE FAMILY

THE GREAT CHINESE
MAGIC FOLD-IN
PUZZLE

A▶

A▶

The crazy puzzle below makes no sense whatso-
ever. But if you carefully fold this page so
that arrows **"A"** meet arrows **"B"** you will see
Magic occur right before your astonished eyes!

◄**B**

◄**B**

HELP A LOSER BECOME A WINNER

Seymour F. Edsel has been a loser all his life. He was placed on a doorstep in a basket as an infant : . . and someone had a change of heart and came back for the basket.

When Seymour finds a wallet, the owner suddenly appears and has him arrested as a pickpocket. When he buys stock it plummets. When he sells, it skyrockets. He just can't win. But now **you** can help Seymour break this terrible cycle. You can help him strike it rich just this once by sending him on the right road to the pot of gold at the end of the rainbow. Please don't let this poor guy down.

ANSWER: If you sent Seymour into the maze to get the pot of gold then he's **still** a loser. Only he's worse off than ever. He'll probably starve to death in there before he realizes that the only **exit** is the **entrance.** So how **do** you get to the pot of gold at the end of the rainbow? If you can't figure that out, maybe you should ask Seymour to move over and make room for another loser. Look again, Dum Dum. The rainbow. What's the matter with the rainbow? Every band leads right to it.

RIDICULOUS RABBIT RIDDLE

One day, in separate parts of the forest, two animals started out in search of dinner. One was a rabbit and the other a bear. "X" marks the spot where they met. But something's wrong. There is only one set of tracks leading **away** from the spot where they met. And those tracks are **rabbit** tracks! But how can that be?

How could a rabbit possibly devour a bear for dinner?

DOTS OF FUN

This time-honored puzzle can be lots of fun if you follow the simple instructions. With crayon or pencil, fill in each space with a dot and a surprise picture will magically appear.

SOLUTION TO DOTS OF FUN

This is the picture you should have gotten if you
followed the instructions ("fill in each space
with a dot"). Of course, some spaces already
had dots so it wasn't necessary to add them
there.

If you got the picture **below,** then you not only
can't follow simple instructions but you missed
out on getting the wonderful surprise picture
all the smarties got. Tough luck, Dum Dum!

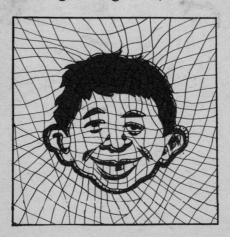

THE MENDACIOUS CUBE TRICK

Here we have a variety of odd shapes. Can you cut them out and arrange them into a cube? This is a toughie so don't be ashamed to give up and look for the answer on the next page.

(Really, we didn't expect you to give up **that** fast!)

ANSWER TO THE MENDACIOUS CUBE TRICK

As we said, this is a toughie! But if you searched carefully, you should have found a cube somewhere. The best and easiest is a child's hollow plastic building block. Then, by simply removing one side, you can easily carry out the instructions for this trick, arranging the cut-out pieces "into a cube."

Some of you may have fallen into the trap of arranging the pieces to form words like **EBUC**, or **BECU**, or **ECUB**, but that's silly because they don't mean anything and besides, what would it have to do with arranging the cut-out pieces into a cube?

A CONNECT-THE-DOTS SURPRISE

Cavalry Scout Seymour Sagebrush has just returned from a dangerous mission into Indian country, with a message of warning. Do you know what it is? Do you know why it's giving Seymour a **splitting** headache? Just when he fervently hoped the soldiers and Indians could bury the **hatchet,** once and for all, Seymour discovers he has an **axe** to grind with the Indians. Know why, huh? Well, stop making wild guesses and start connecting dots so you, too, will know exactly what's **on Seymour's mind!**

THE TANTAL-EYES-ZING MAGIC SPOT TRICK

In the center of this page there is a spot. If you will stare at it for one full hour, something astounding will occur. Slowly but surely the spot will split into two distinctly separate images. But remember you must stare at the spot for a **full hour.** Anything less and all you'll see is the *single spot shown here.

*Please note: A few rare people will see two spots right from the start. This is indicative of a specific eye disorder that should not be further aggravated by doing this trick. Besides, why would anyone with an incurable and fatal eye disease want to bother with silly tricks, anyway?

THE PREPOSTEROUS
PYRAMID PUZZLER

Archaeologist Digby Shovelshot has apparently discovered a new pyramid. From the facts given below, can you tell how much earth Professor Shovelshot will have to remove in order to reveal his fantastic discovery to the world?

Assuming that this new pyramid is the same size as the old one in the background, here are the dimensions to work with: The base is 755 feet 2½ inches on all four sides, the height is 451 feet 1⅞ inches.

SOLUTION TO
PREPOSTEROUS PYRAMID PUZZLER

Professor Shovelshot has no more digging to do. What he has found is the tippy-tippy top stone of the pyramid in the background.

CHAPTER ELEVEN

TRICK SHOTS
FOR LITTLE SHOTS
OR
GUN FOR THE
WHOLE FAMILY

118

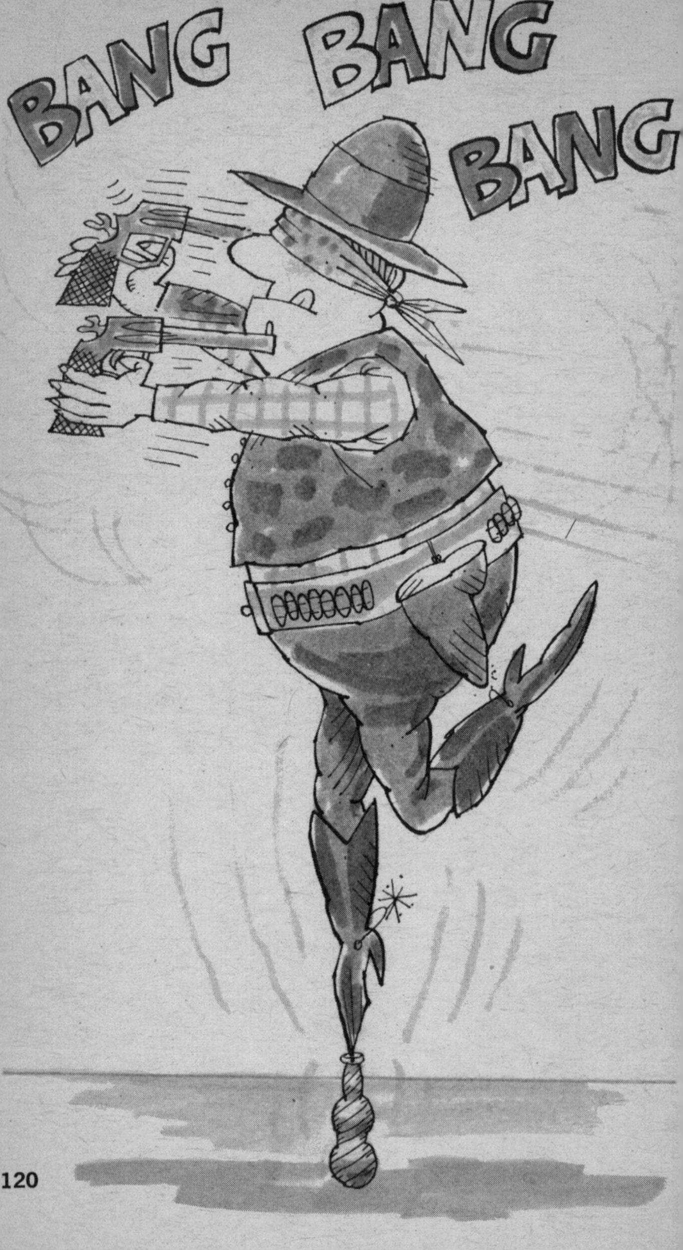
BANG
BANG
BANG

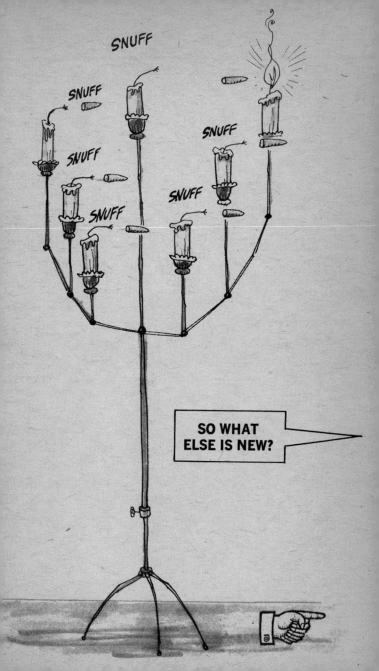

CHAPTER TWELVE

MORE (YECCH!) ADVANCED TRICKS FOR ADVANCED CLODS

OR

IN ADVANCE OF MORE ADVANCED MYSTICISM THAT WOULD CERTAINLY PROVE TOO ADVANCED FOR YOU IF WE HADN'T PREPARED YOU FOR THE BIG TIME, SO WELL IN ADVANCE

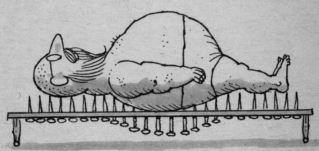

THE CLASSIC GOOSE
LAYING THE GOLDEN EGG TRICK

MORAL: The person who insists on the best usually has to take a lot of other stuff before he gets it.

Yet another eggstravagant chapter (yycch!) due.

THE HISTRIONIC
"PICK A CARD" TRICK

Fan out a deck of cards. Ask someone in your audience to pick a card and replace it in your deck. Pretend to concentrate and strain for twenty or thirty minutes to build up suspense. Then, when the strain seems almost too unbearable, start to deal out the cards slowly. To everyone's utter delight and reverence, you will stop and identify the correct card.

HOW THE TRICK IS DONE

This is an extremely involved trick but it gave delight and got you reverence, didn't it? So, the illustrations on the following art page show exactly what is needed to effectively crown this trick with deserved glory and triumph.

131

Assistant is planted in audience with powerful binoculars . . .

After he spots card picked, he notes it and sneaks out.

In a back room he sends message . . . by teletype.

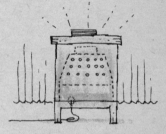

Message arrives on teletype in magician's table.

It's got to be the card following the Ace of clubs!

Card's identity is reflected into mirror in magician's ring.

Magician names card and silences heckler with magic wand.

THE LANGUID
"CUTTING AND RESTORING" TRICK

Ask a man in your audience for his tie. This trick is particularly effective if it's a very **expensive** tie. Now, whip out a pair of shears and deftly snip the tie in two. Of course, your volunteer will either attempt to kill you or cry like a baby. Or both. This can be dangerous and disgusting and should be avoided. Thus, quickly assure him that you will magically restore his tie to one piece. Place each half of the tie in a different pocket of your jacket. Then, pretend to strain and sweat for as long as you feel necessary to build suspense. Suddenly, after exclaiming "Cravat, cravat . . . in two seconds flat!", you pull the tie out . . . in ONE PIECE!

HOW THE TRICK IS DONE

Your real hands are actually inside dummy rubber ones that are attached to your sleeves. After you put the tie halves into your pockets, you withdraw your hands inside your coat where you have concealed needle and thread. Through openings on the inside of your pockets you reach in and get the tie halves. It is then a simple matter to sew the tie halves together during the time you pretend to strain and sweat. Only you're not pretending. If you think sewing under these conditions is a snap, just try it sometime. Anyway, when you're finished, replace the tie in a pocket and you're ready to conclude the trick.

Fake rubber hand

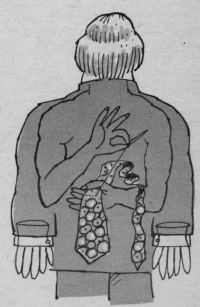

THE BRAZEN BLADE
"MAGNETIC KNIFE" TRICK

Hold up what looks like an ordinary table knife for your audience to see. Tell them that your body contains the special magic power of magnetism. To prove it, you grasp the knife in your clenched fist. Say a few magic words and . . . **PRESTO** . . . when you open your fist the knife remains stuck to your hand, no matter how violently you wave it around.

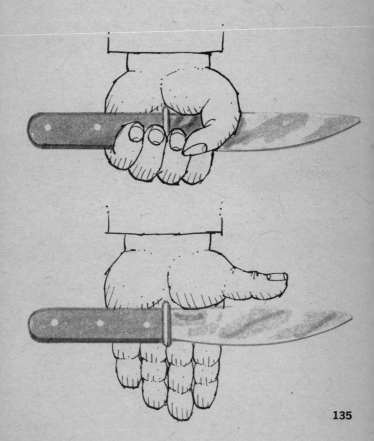

HOW THE TRICK IS DONE

Naturally, the business of magnetism in your body is a lot of baloney, even though some people say you have a "magnetic personality" or "animal magnetism". The trick here is a specially designed knife in which the blade part slides forward to reveal two needle-sharp prongs. When placing the knife in the hand you simply clamp the prongs into the fleshy part of your hand. Thus, the most violent waving of the hand can't possibly dislodge it.

NOTE: Practice not wincing when you drive the prongs home. Also take care not to strike a vein as the resultant gush of blood will obviously spoil the trick.

Needle-sharp prongs

CHAPTER THIRTEEN

THE SCATHING KNIFE-THROWING TRICK
OR
STUCK AGAIN

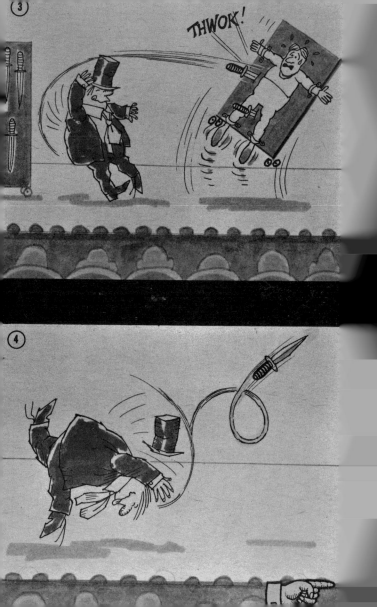

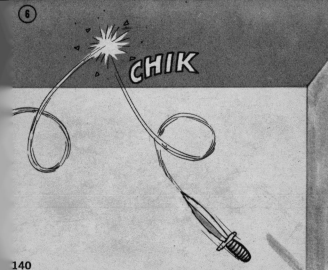

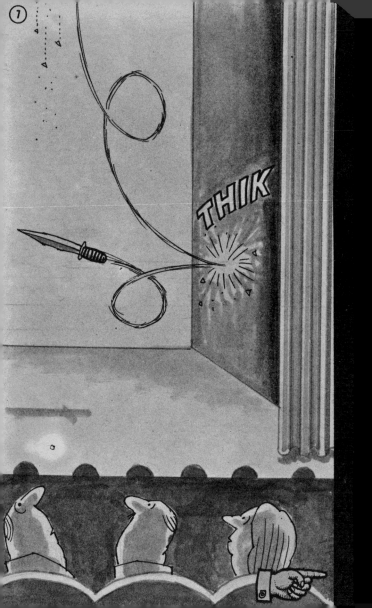

CHAPTER FOURTEEN

THE GREAT BUMBLEONI'S UNFORGETTABLE MEMORY FEAT OR OR OR OR OR... ER...OR OR...

STAGE DOOR

THE GREAT MBLEONI

CHAPTER FIFTEEN

THE IMPOSSIBLE
CAMEL TRICK
OR
THE MOST
UNHEARD OF THING
YOU EVER HEARD OF!

THE IMPOSSIBLE
"CAMEL THROUGH THE EYE OF A NEEDLE" TRICK

For centuries, the saying "like putting a camel through the eye of a needle" has been used to express the impossible. But now at last we can lay that old myth to rest. Here we have a camel, right? And there we have a needle, right? So, now let us proceed . . .

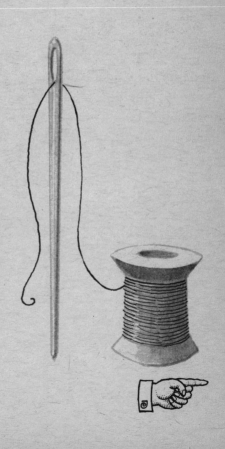

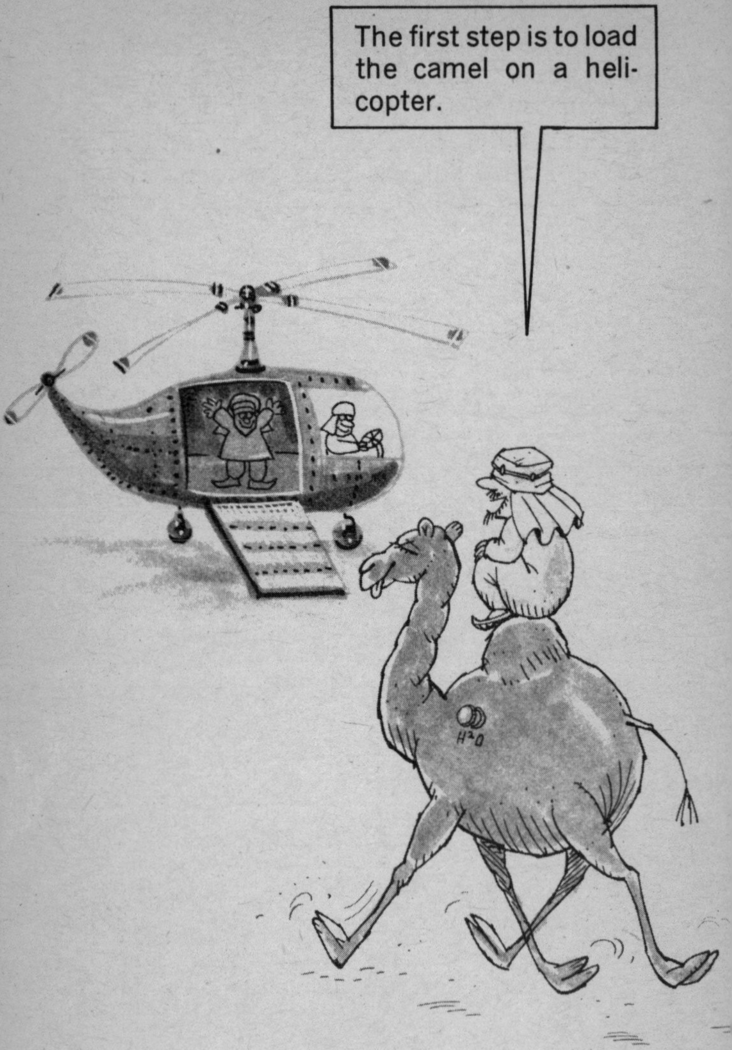
The first step is to load the camel on a helicopter.
H^2O

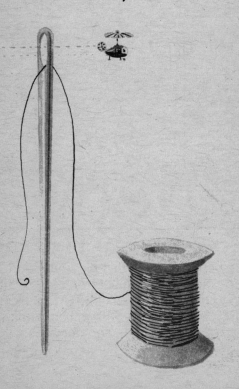

FIND THE "ONE BIG MISTAKE" PUZZLE

There is just **one big mistake** in this picture. Can you find it? We know that after hours of frustration, you'll be sorely tempted to give up. If you stick to it, we're sure you'll find the result rewarding. If you give up, you'll find it even more rewarding.

ANSWER TO THE "ONE BIG MISTAKE" PUZZLE

The one big mistake in this picture is that it is the wrong picture. This one is for a puzzle titled "CAN YOU FIND THE 3,749 MISTAKES IN THIS PICTURE?". The picture with only one mistake in it somehow got put into another book.

CHAPTER SIXTEEN

PHANTASTIC PHENOMENA
OR
PHUN PHOR THE
WHOLE FAMILY

THE CARPET

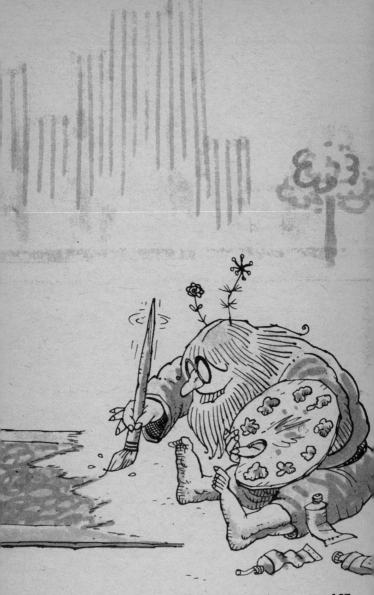

THE ROPE

170

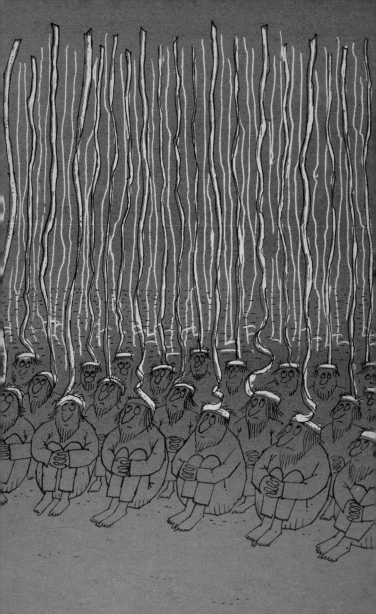

CHAPTER
SEVENTEEN

**IN A VAST NATIONWIDE
PRE-PUBLICATION POLL,
THIS CHAPTER
WAS BY FAR
THE MOST POPULAR
ONE IN THE BOOK.**

CHAPTER EIGHTEEN

AT LAST
THE LAST OF (YECCH!)
ADVANCED TRICKS
FOR ADVANCED CLODS
OR
FOR A REAL
DIRTY TRICK,
DO SOMETHING NICE
TO A MASOCHIST

THE CLASSIC GOOSE
LAYING THE GOLDEN EGG TRICK

MORAL: When you think you've given all you've got there's still a little more.

At last, no more of this eggravating (ycch!) stuff!

THE PERNICIOUS "FORCED CARD" TRICK

Have a member of your audience name a card. Reach into your pocket, produce a deck, and ask him to pick a card. To everyone's complete astonishment, it will be the card he named.

HOW THE TRICK IS DONE

This trick is foolproof provided you have a good memory. The cards in the deck you produced in the foregoing trick were all the same so no matter what card the man picked, it had to be the one he named. "Ah", you say testily, "But what if he had named another card?" Well, here's where the good memory part comes in. Concealed on your person are **fifty-two** decks, each deck containing fifty-two of the **same** card. All you have to do is remember where the right deck is after a card is named.

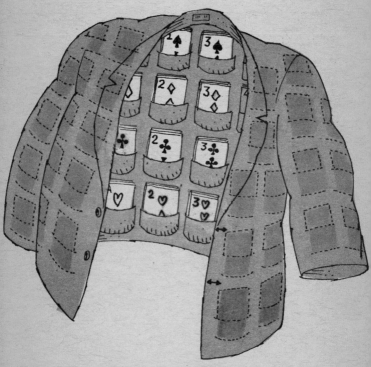

THE STYLISH
"BREAKING A TWO BY FOUR IN HALF WITH A DOLLAR BILL" TRICK

Fold a dollar bill in half the long way. Keep "sharpening" the crease and stress this fact to your audience, utilizing jokes about how sharp and sturdy it's got to be to chop anything as tough as a two by four in half. Then wind up and with one swift blow rend the plank asunder.

HOW THE TRICK IS DONE

As you bring the dollar bill down, quickly insert your forefinger in the crease. Thus, unbeknownst to the audience, it is not really the bill that cuts the plank in half but your finger. It is wise to anesthetize the finger beforehand. If this is not possible, then keep a small rubber ball in your mouth so that you can bite down on it till the unbearably excruciating pain subsides. You'll be ready for your next plank within two weeks or so.

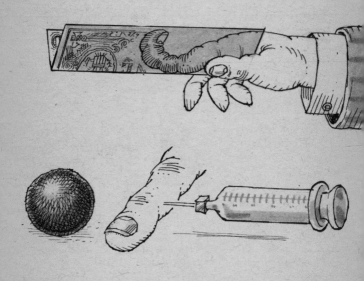

THE HILARIOUS "PRACTICAL JOKE" TRICK

Ask for a volunteer from the audience and bet him a **dollar** you can do all of the following tricks . . .

(A) Throw a dozen eggs at him without breaking a single one.

(B) Shave his head with a razor without disturbing a single hair.

(C) Snip his tie with scissors and then make it whole again.

(D) Set fire to his wallet and restore it completely.

(E) Drop a bowling ball on his foot without causing any pain or swelling.

(F) Pour sulfuric acid over his entire body without inflicting any damage.

HOW IT IS DONE:

It is not! How in the world could it be? But so what! How else can you have so much fun for a **buck...?** And your audience will love it. That is if they don't die of old age waiting for a volunteer to appear who is stupid enough to take this bet.

THE CUMULATIVE "BRASS RING" TRICK

Let the audience examine a small brass ring to prove that it is solid. Then place the ring on your head and cover it with a kerchief. Moments later you remove the kerchief and reveal the astonishing fact that the ring is now tightly around your neck.

HOW THE TRICK IS DONE

You'll need a lot of greasy kid stuff on your hair for this one. Also, your hair should be long enough to touch your collar so that a pair of cables can be hidden in it. These cables run down your sleeves and end as loop-shaped cuff links. What happens is this: When you place the brass ring on your head you deftly hook a cable to each side. Then, while engaging the audience in light banter, you also secretly engage the cuff link loops to hooks sticking out of two holes in the table. These hooks lead to powerful motor-driven winches which pull the brass ring down over your head with the equivalent of about three tons of pressure.

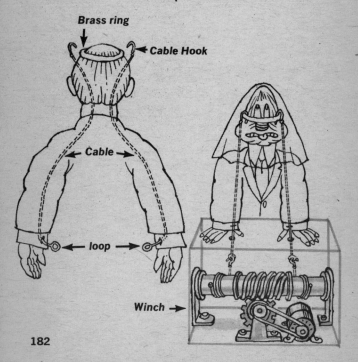

Brass ring

Cable Hook

Cable

loop

Winch

CHAPTER NINETEEN

THE GREAT BUMBLEONI'S LAST STAND OR AREN'T YOU GLAD THIS IS THE FINAL CHAPTER IN THE BOOK? WE CERTAINLY ARE!

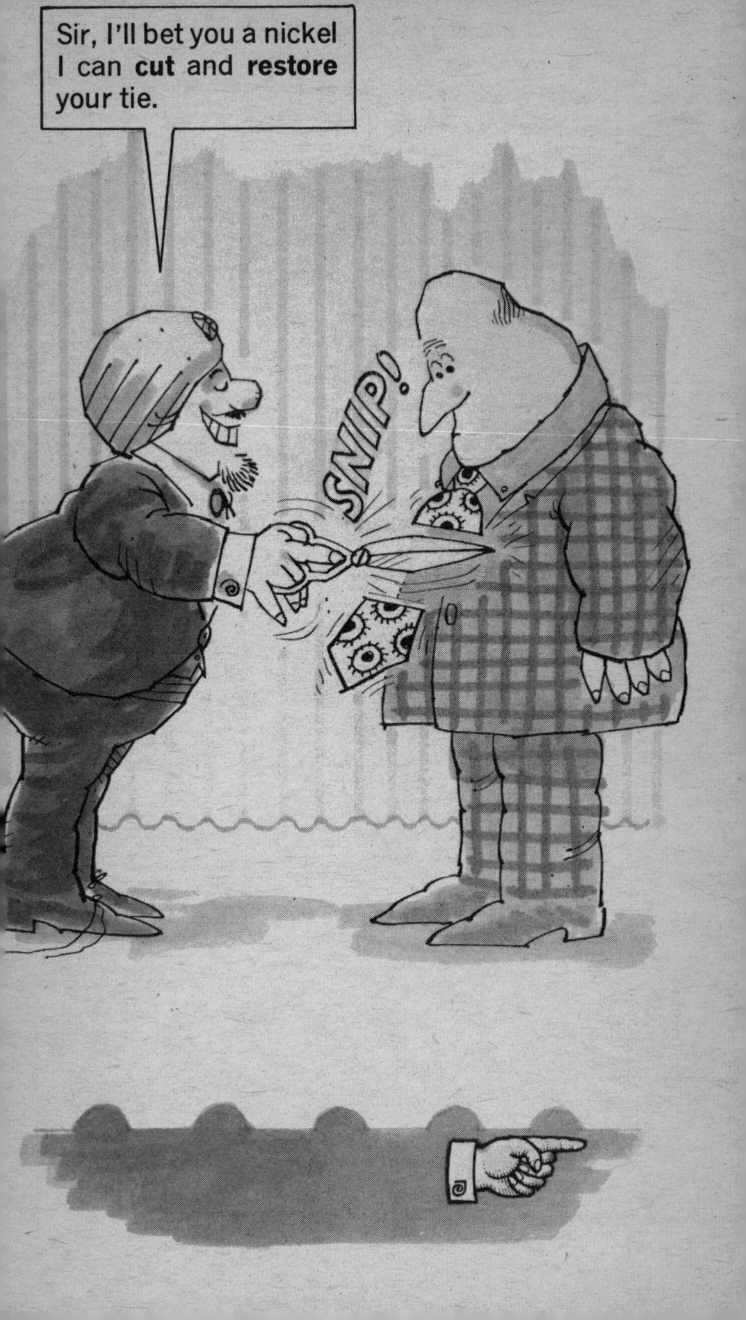

Sir, I'll bet you a nickel I can **cut** and **restore** your tie.
SNIP!